Unspoken

Kimberly Roy

BookLeaf Publishing

India | USA | UK

Presentation by *BookLeaf Publishing*

Web: www.bookleafpub.com

E-mail: info@bookleafpub.com

ISBN: 9789357213769

First edition 2022

POEM 1

The loose end, does it tie?
Only today did I notice I am the one
With answers to:
Preventions of loops fastening.
Somewhere the answer must lie
With truth, the unknown, the tie-
That which I cannot change,
I therefore must cry
Accepting the unknown
Pronouncing my own truths for destiny
Gone with confusion, confuse-ectomy.
There is only one of me and I believe
Happiness eventually greets
Prevailing souls.
Always have I been
Collective until then
Chaos leaves laces untied
Becoming a bountiful being
Beckons one string to each side.

POEM 2

2

Mark my words with intent to distribute
Count on the times I used to care
Why would you, though?
Pitch black in corners of a coiled stomach
I crouched.

Tiny disbursements of chance
Rang out, it swallowed doubt
Until the right way to put it made cents worth
spending,
Not sense worth making.
Like an Indian Sunburn it churned raw the heat
source.
What is it?

POEM 3

Diamond in the rough
I could clean-up without passion
But it of course would just be an act
I should get all of this off my chest-

No shame
I won't change
Even when you rip my page
Never tied my own noose
I am not good with loops
A third-eye radar
No wandering away
Typing blunt
Keyboard, my ashtray

Plants grow back but the soul remains tangled
Oreo kitty with them fangs that dangle
Feral to any system
Is the roof for my kittens
Please, don't make me leave!
When I can't find my mittens.
Playing along until the pieces come together
But I am not a follower
Working these jobs beneath Babylon
Is the only father I ever had: time

The only sun I ever saw: shine

4

POEM 4

I don't wanna complain about what I don't have-
When I can still heal through a good laugh-

Down on the low in traffic with the trucks
Barely aware I'm thuggin' through the muck
People waiting to see me at the top
Anyone who's met me knows that I won't stop.
First impression
We probably aren't meshing
Second wavelength we feel each other's
strength.
Crave more and say less
Stress no more, we gotta score.
We gotta score.

Princess on her throne
Higher than a drone
Always been a lyricist
I get It on my own.
Starved to death, not right nor left.

A friend for a stint took the wheel of her whip
And said she was good but began to slip
Then it flipped with her Pontiac that same
Summer

When I was like, Turn right, she told me Don't
be a bummer.
Sped up instead, steal did bend.
Didn't want an impound
Gas pedal and top down
Climbed out the passenger's side
Cuz the driver's side inground.

POEM 5

I feel warmer when I see
Outside my windows, an arm's reach from the
porch-
Confusion at first glance.
Where are my glasses?
Color-blind, though-
I am not.
A puddle-shaped prism prematurely pokes
eyesight adjusting.
Just sting.
Interesting…
I see the freezing cold, and therefore-
I am not.

POEM 6

Hungering for comfort
The cupboards do not appease me
There are not cupcakes in the pantry
There is no Gatorade on the porch
But I stocked up on things to
Wipe my face when I cry about it.

Who do I think I am?
I do matter, as long as I have matter
In fact, you would drown in my depths
Just like me-
Just like me-
But I stocked up on floats
We can all use together.

I know all about
The train station
You do, too
But not like me.
An owl, a crow, but not much the morning type
The white city van is followed by a cop
The train is coming; run.

Some of us can see and if not
Hope, conceptualize

To understand
But for the rest
More than Some
There are only other people.
Herds of sheep
And I love sheep
But I prefer fellow herders
When spilling tea on our scarves.

Moderation, comfort, joy
In sequence with good health
Worth and prosperity,
Paths to friends and family.
There are no directions
But if there are
The English version got lost in the mail-
Christmas Season.
A challenge
I am hungry to devour
And eager to assemble.

POEM 7

Described as such- perfect
Only when the stone wall it
Helps complete compelling drivers
Speeding by two-hundred years later in
Machines great with mass, force,
And complexion-
Perplex a set of observations from expressions
Of a soul old enough to notice most sturdy a
spot-
Fitted tight as a bolt fits its screw
A sense allotted
A rock carried by no one
The brick there holding so much of this wall
Still stretching until crumbling away
With the signs of new millennials
Again.

POEM 8

But afraid to sleep.

I am sorry, young girl, for the troubles ahead
I am sorry for treating everything like nothing
As if you did not exist,
As if you do not still live.

I have not stopped thinking about you
Since the idea was brought to my attention
Need not say how,
Progressed is my desire to address you:

Young girl, like the poem you will love someday
Young girl, I am sorry for what you will do to
yourself
For consequences make you stop.
I had no intention on saying sorry, young girl, as
I was you-

I had no intentions at all but to write
Choked by suppression of my own possession
Realms to my soul facing oppression.
Impulsive, we have to slow down, still.
We still have to do that, slow down.

Some things are miraculous
Some things are quaint
By connecting the dots, your scabs will clot.

Mercury stamps you.
Please, stop-
Going into regret mode.

She will not die, but she will suffer longer than
hard feelings.
I cannot tell her yet, or ever for that matter.
I am here now. I have made it.

POEM 9

I just talk out loud to him
Sometimes, when I feel his presence-
Sometimes. In my bedroom
He wanted to hear my voice
But I lost it.

Weeping over
Drastic measures for
My everything.

Random attacks
Smack my back, kicked
Down more than out-
Overcoming myself is the truest battle.

I think he tries
To tear the note off
Since now
Behind me.

To heal, find solace in knowing
The future is mine to declare.

Every day is not with him

And I would love to love
Again.

He came by tonight-
Sacred in a flash
I saw a secret stash.

I know it is you-
I know it is you.
Ziplocked in heaven
I love you, too.

POEM 10

When she sprang into action
Because one thing led to another
One being learns from the mother
And I hurt because she hurt.

For getting into trouble write not
Poorly of the hand that fed you.

Finding a road block
Causing fear
But I cannot control that sphere
Everything I know revolves around
You
Including me.

I find it hard to write
I found it hard to write
I am finding you hard to say
You find me hard to love
You found me hard to love
But you always do nonetheless-
I found you less than I wanted to, too
But more than I could ask for
Which I did not
Because once I knew

Was more than I expected
By the time it was too late
To get eight hours of sleep.

It was never too late
The wind always carried away burdens unheard
There was always enough
The sky was not shy to slow-burn a crescent.

POEM 11

I spoke aloud today
In many different ways
Portrayed myself as such.

I read aloud today
So, she could never say
I lost my voice.

Today she spoke aloud
Explaining different ways to see
Through bite marks in bologna.

Hopping on driftwood
I could sleep with both eyes open
And listening.

POEM 12

Pain is the symptom of pain
And to heal is a result of
I hate to say trying harder but
If you did it so many times before
Why can you not learn from that
And do it bigger and professionally
More than ever before, again?

Pain is living on the third floor and not having
any clean undies to wear,
Nor any work pants since apparently,
I need to be in the office for my remote job
The next day.
It was supposed to be over by now.

Today sucked because
Yesterday was fantastical
Family operations are questionable
There are surface people and loyal people.
Each person's values discern their lane
Where to each their own is hardly accepted.

Pain is the misery of having to do the laundry
As later and later it gets,

Somebody in this building must be using it
already
And I should have gone earlier.
I would feel a lot better
With clean clothes and sheets
And towels, though, oh!

I suppose I could get a couple loads together
And toss them over the balcony
In a laundry bag
If the ground isn't wet.
Otherwise, I will satisfy finally
My mental affliction with not ever existing
My jokes are a preexisting condition.
I am so tired, though!

Suppose I redo the make-up I cried off a couple
hours ago
During that movie I wrote about
For I may not remember otherwise.
Writing is something I can no longer give up and
walk away from
They call it a living room but a lot of dreams die
in them.

Suppose I take a nap, then revisit my options
Suppose I work through, all the exhaustion.

The wood floors are long planks of caramel hard
candies
Stamped with knots, nails, and grains.
How do I put into frame a feeling
Crushing a squirming heart?
The fires in my chest are wild
My throat a lounge for tightness interfering
No entry allowed
My whole being is cautious.

POEM 13

No expectations, not even for today
I left my guard at the door for some holiday.

After-afternoon, when I was well-within my
year
Wonder what reminded her- the dusk, the night,
or fear?
Thin, purple air with light-streak sank
She called me then, the gift I thank.

I love her always but did not always.

A timeless bond to heal with time
Today her truth makes me not mind
I said to us, I am not bothered for I hold my own
But ice melts quick on sorrow; two hearts, one
milestone.

POEM 14

Waking up unable to breathe soundly. Physical
symptoms:
Internal sadness ruptures stress into
Volcanic chest, Pompeii
Will I be like this forever?
Achiness in my heart
Hating the feeling of internal organs
Squeamish kicking around what gets bad-
Waiting for my body to rip itself apart.
But at the same time: relieved if it could already.
And I can't stop moving;
Mind nor body
My soul.

Stress knots in back acting up
Neck mobility.
Achy stress I cannot eliminate until it is too late
Even though I want to, as bad as it hurts
An anxious heart, racing time.

Doubtful mind after mind
Running in circles
Panic amounts
And a room begins to rot
Art supplies to organize

Make everything have a spot
Defeated soon without a doubt
I come forth and back to mount.

POEM 15

Tolerant to the virtual fires set in my soul
Intolerant to waking up
Reality does not doze away
Reality does not hear you pray.

Nurtures dreams to be natural
Uncontrolled but lucid I step
Projecting my body afloat until
Inanimate objects stop me.

It is hard to be a waitress in such a small
restaurant
On sea sometimes not being able to steer
yourself
But I have worked at just one
Realistically, though, I suppose two.

I have an apartment downtown
And in the same neighborhood another
But sometimes I live in the house from my
childhood
And other times, many times
I am outside looking for
My person, not my home.

POEM 16

Christmas is canceled this two-thousand-twenty
Hidden to be recovered
Values reset, reevaluated, resurrected
Trees prone more to love and longevity
Ever are the greens a lasting species
But are they so solid a breed?
The rediscovery of Christmas Eve
One sour essence comes to mind
With butterflies wild within-
Telling you something
You know about him.

POEM 17

I am a writing artist
You won't take that from me
I have suffered under false pretense
For long as can be
When needing to tell you off is
The actual necessity.

In fact, it should be a commodity.
There is no more time
There are no more hurdles
There are no more tricks that will flip this over
Now I concur everything I have already known.

POEM 18

How dreams cause your body instinctually to
react-
Is the reality, in fact, of how you really feel.
I may only speak of my own accord foretelling
What is and is not scientific enough, for some.

For instance, I woke up this morning:
The end of a dream it seemed the deceased
And my uncle, perhaps, teamed-up
Revengeful fun in those kinds of eyes.
The last thing I remember:
The wings of a plane like a prehistoric bird
Painted all white
Soared downwards with its swords
Into an invisible drain
When suddenly-
And I was looking at this uncontrollable matter
From the hold of a still far from shore tube
So as not to have an ability to duck.
The remnants of the big, white plane turned
sideways
Plunged towards the tree-tops
Over our beloved camp
It looked like recycled parts.

Shaking ink still I hold
The crash we could not see
But, by logic know it happened
Very deep inside of me.
It was like being susceptible to pneumonia,
Wet and shivering like that waking up.
Convulsions were here. Graffiti.
Havoc stuck to my skin.
Physiologically-
Something happened to my body when I was not
there!

POEM 19

This is a writing pen among all of them
The felt would have dried up in between
Lines of bleeding letters made to blur.
The gel draws beautifully
But leaves its own blotted mark.
I make the dots here
To be continued.

The decision to use this writing pen among all of
them
Was better suited as a segway to the page
Than the page was an open gate
Remaining stagnant, staring blankly.

Never had I noticed it there
The only utensil I would choose to write with
And so, I am writing with the pen suited
Best among them to deliver finery-
And not let another empty page lead to another...

From now on, this pen does the talking.

POEM 20

I dropped out of college (clean)
Pause. Optimism.
Then failed out twice more (dirty)
Pause. Sick to your stomach.

That is kind of what happens
When one becomes a writer
A real one
Who writes.

You know-
I tend to not right anything
Until necessary.

This journey has a webbed past
I did not plan
Nor plan on planning anyways
But I can sweep how the restaurant taught me
And, we cool.

Brooks sparkle
Flowing edges softens
Moss reaching to hug more rocks
And spots on boulders.

Every day is hard to breathe and look at but
I was not born this way.
I have alterations to my psyche from growing up
With heightened senses
Hyperaware and afraid of the unexpected.
I admit I was afraid.

I held myself close, though.
I slept through hovering breath,
Did I not?
I wished so much to lash out at the human-
The human who brought me here
To lay in a stiff, cold bed
With spiders around the duvet; stiff covers.

I feared her and loathed her at the same time
Relying on her to survive
Until free-
I have failed.
But at the same time
Have I survived and yet to conquer.

POEM 21

I am wicked shaky but believe I can still write
Every motorcycle today can eat shit.
"How He Hurt Me" is going to be about:
Not wanting to go outside anymore
My body, I paid no mind to
Was it how I hurt myself?
I chose to hold on
No one did that for me
"How He Hurt Me" is a messy place.
I want to envision myself
As I once used to see:
Healthy, self- disciplined
I saw me for who I could be
In the airy apartment downtown
Outstretched on a yoga mat pointing
Fingertips to the ceiling.
And here I am, in the place with the things
And the scenes all me, my world.
Yet I am crippled and weak with tension
Shaking like a plucked guitar string.